Emmanuel
A Christmas Devotional

MAGGIE GREENWAY

DEDICATION

I dedicate this book to my Dad, Rick Hoover. His gritty
faith in the middle of a thirty-year battle with Multiple
Sclerosis will always be my inspiration.

EMMANUEL

INTRODUCTION

Welcome to the Christmas season! While this season can be so sweet and memory-rich, it can also be a sprint, bouncing from one event and task to another. My prayer is that this little devotional would help you to find moments in this busy season to focus on who is present WITH us as we flit from mall to market to memory. Jesus was born over two thousand years ago to be with us, to walk among us, to understand us, and to eventually rescue us so that we can forever be with him. Bottom line: we are not alone. Our God is with us.

The next twenty-four days are a journey through the Bible from beginning to end of where God declares his Presence with his people. Let's journey to discover the heart of our God who forever dwells with us.

Each day includes a scripture, a reflection, a prayer, and a digging deeper question. If you would like to push yourself, take some time to answer these questions in a journal.

I am so excited for you to seek to deeply understand how God is present with us! Let's get started!

DECEMBER 1

The virgin

shall conceive

and bear a son,

and shall call

his name

Emmanuel.

Isaiah 7:14

The month to focus on Christ's coming into the world as a newborn baby, on God wrapping himself in human flesh, taking on our vulnerabilities, our brokenness, to save us…not just in the blink of an eye. He chose to walk our world for three decades. The name of God Emmanuel means just that "God with Us".

Isaiah, in this scripture, prophecies Jesus' coming to be with us. Emmanuel: God with us. Those three words speak volumes of who Jesus is.

- GOD with us: He is fully God, Divine.
- God WITH us: He is present, actively engaged
- God with US: It is for humanity that he became a person just like us.

Let's spend this month, digging deeper into how God has been our Emmanuel since the start and how he continues to do that even into our age!

Daily Prayer:
Father, people of our time are hurting with so much pain, sickness, and suffering. We need to know we are not alone in this life. We need to have you with us, your power, and your understanding. We beg you to stay with us, to never leave us. We need you, our Creator, our Almighty God. Thank you for sending Jesus, to fulfill this prophecy, born of a virgin, to be Emmanuel, God with us. Open our hearts to know what that means for us this Christmas season. Draw us even closer into your arms.

Digging Deeper:
What do you think it must have been like for God to become a person?

DECEMBER 2

The LORD appeared to
Isaac and said,
"Do not go down to
Egypt; live in the land
where I tell you to live.
Stay in this land a while,
and I will be with you
and will bless you."
Genesis 26:3

When famine strikes the land, Isaac plans to take his family to Egypt where they could find abundant food. It makes perfect sense. But God has other plans and appears to Isaac to let him know Egypt is not the answer. If he trusts God and stays where God tells him, God promises to be with him and bless him. When God is with his people, his blessings seem to overflow. For Isaac, God provides abundantly for their physical needs during this time of famine. He finds well after well of water and reaps a crop one hundred-fold what was sown. God's hand of blessing is clearly on him.

It's been in my hardest "famine" times when circumstances were the worst, that God has showed himself more present with me than ever. I desperately leaned hard into Jesus, the only Rock of Refuge who satisfies (trust me I tried others!). God provided strength beyond myself; he provided financially; he put a supportive community around me, but most of all, I rested in the comfort of his presence, knowing he understood my pain even if no one else could.

Daily Prayer:
Lord, we, like Isaac, need your Presence. Help us not to run to what seems like a quick fix, but to trust you even when we don't quite understand your leading. Thank you that with you are endless gifts of all kinds. Thank you for understanding each of our hearts and minds and bodies.

Digging Deeper:
What does this passage reveal to us about the character of God? What names could you give him based on his relationship with Isaac?

DECEMBER 3

I am
with you
and will watch
over you
wherever you go.
Genesis 28:15

Turn the page in your Bible from where we were yesterday and we see God promising his presence again, this time to Jacob who is on his way to hideout at his Uncle's place. He tricked his brother Esau and now runs away to avoid revenge. In the middle of his fleeing, he falls asleep on a rock (I've always found that odd!). God speaks with him while he sleeps and promises to keep the covenant he had promised to Jacob's father Isaac and grandfather Abraham. God promises to be with Jacob and watch over him wherever he goes.

As he fell asleep that night, I imagine Jacob was afraid for his life, vulnerable out in the open. God meets him right where he is the most at risk. God promises to watch over him and to be with him. As an adult, do you ever long to be a kid again and have a loving adult take care of you? I long to rest into a strong protector. Wouldn't that be comforting?! With God, we can. He watches over us. His Presence is nearer than our breathe. Let's lean into him as our good, watchful Father today.

Daily Prayer:
Lord God, thank you for watching over us. Thank you for the security your presence brings. Help us today to run to you in our times of struggle. Remind us through the day of your palpable presence. Lord bring rest over each of us as we pray, helping us to lean back into your arms of protection today.

Digging Deeper:
In this section of scripture, what does God reveal about himself?

DECEMBER 4

Then the LORD
said to Jacob,
"Go back to
the land of
your fathers
and to your relatives,
and I will be
with you."
Genesis 31:3

We are hanging out with Jacob again today. Decades have passed. He now has 11 sons and several daughters from four wives. He still lives in his Uncle Laban's household where he's worked since he ran away from home years before. God is clearly with him. His flocks increased while Laban's decreased. Jacob anxiously notices his Uncle's and cousins' jealousy. At that time God once again intervenes. God tells Jacob to finally head home and reassures him that he would continue with him.

I love how human Jacob is. After this great reassurance from the Almighty God, Jacob packs up all his possessions and wives and children and heads out while his Uncle is out of town. I can so relate. Can't you? We have all these amazing promises for us in the Bible about grace, salvation, God's presence with us, and yet, I so commonly hear God and half obey, half self-protect just in case. Laban eventually meets up with Jacob to say a peaceful good-bye to his daughters and grandchildren. Even with his sneaky lack of trust, God still continues on with Jacob, blessing him not only with provision but also with resolution in his relationship with Laban and eventually with his brother as well.

Daily Prayer:

Emmanuel, we need your help to continue in trust today. Thank you for your grace when we make a mess of our own way in our attempt to "help" your plan like Jacob did. Thank you for staying close to us through your Holy Spirit. Thank you for your Word and our ability to read your words every single day rather than waiting for decades for you to speak like Jacob did.

Digging Deeper:

In what way is this section of scripture particularly meaningful to you today?

DECEMBER 5

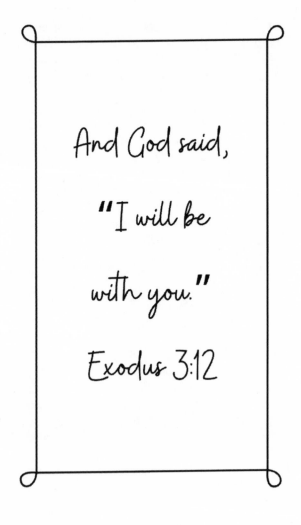

And God said,

"I will be

with you."

Exodus 3:12

I love how humbly Moses begins his leadership. The mighty man of God who God will use to perform miracle after miracle, whose face will shine from being in God's glory…this same man begs God to send someone else at the start.

God speaks to Moses from the burning bush to call him to be the voice of a compassionate God to his oppressed people. God has come to deliver them and bring them to the promise land…a promise that began more than four hundred years before. From the hindsight we now have, it seems silly that Moses would beg to not go. However, I can totally relate. He ran from Egypt forty years before and has lived peacefully and in obscurity as a shepherd. He started a family and has settled down. It's hard to leave what's known and comfortable. God promises Emmanuel. "I will be with you." It's this promise and that of sending his brother with him that finally calms Moses into agreement. He will not be alone on this adventure…The Almighty God who Sees goes with him.

Today, let's trust that like Moses, God goes with us where he calls us. He sees our struggles; he knows our hearts; he understands our weaknesses and insecurities, and he promises to never leave.

Daily Prayer:
Father, thank you for seeing our suffering and not leaving us alone in it. Thank you that just as you saw your people enslaved and delivered them, you will break the bonds of our slavery to addiction, to false securities, to unhealthy relationships. Lord, as we walk into the call you've placed in each of our hearts, thank you for the promise of being near us.

Digging Deeper:
In what way do you relate to Moses here?

DECEMBER 6

My Presence

will go with you

and

I will give you rest.

Exodus 33:14

Israel is free of their bondage to Egypt, but in their desert wanderings, they quickly fall into the slavery of idol worship. Moses has climbed a mountain to meet with God. He's been gone so long the people believe he's not returning. They make a golden calf to worship. How quickly we replace God with something more tangible and convenient when waiting on the Lord seems to take forever. Who's feeling the conviction here? I know I am.

Well, God's anger burns toward the people and he declares to Moses that he will not continue with them or he would surely kill the people. Now, Moses is desperate and begs the LORD to remain with them. God hears Moses's prayer and promises to remain with the people and give them rest.

Our confidence comes not from our own ability to grit out the path before us. Confidence comes from Jesus, who like Moses, goes to the Father for us and intercedes for us. He is our perfect bridge to God. He can relate to our struggles and pain, and yet he is the perfect Son of God. He intercedes for us sinful people more powerfully than Moses could. More than that, he died in our place and rose again to conquer death itself. Today we can enter God's throne room and receive the grace and mercy.

Daily Prayer:
Father, thank you for going with us in life. Help us today to put down the idols that so easily tempt us to question you or give up on you. Thank you that we have soul rest because Jesus took our punishment for us and brings us to your Throne of grace.

Digging Deeper:
Does this passage address an issue with which you struggle? What truth can you take away from this section to help you in your area of need?

DECEMBER 7

I will walk among you and be your God, and you will be my people.

Leviticus 26:12

In this part of the Old Testament, after explaining the laws of Holy Living to the Hebrews, God begins to recite his blessings for them. I love these words…I will walk among you. Years and years before Christ, we have a picture of his walking in our shoes, along our roads, among us. God came near. God placed his dwelling with us…first in his tent of worship, then in Christ being with us, and finally through his Holy Spirit making his home in our hearts.

The second part of this verse speaks to me of belonging. I think we all long to be part of something that matters…a family, a team, a relationship, a company, a church… When we uproot and no longer feel our security in belonging to whatever we were a part, we feel lost and long to latch onto something new. The God of our souls knows this need and I think he also has this need. Over and over in the Old Testament, God repeats…I will be your God and you will be my people. We belong to God. That part makes sense…he is our creator. The next part blows my mind…HE BELONGS TO US! The God of the entire universe, the Almighty, the Creator, he is ours. We belong to him, more than the company for which we work, the church we attend, or the friends we have. We belong to God Almighty and He belongs to us. That speaks to me of a security that deeply satisfies.

Daily Prayer:
Father God, you are our Creator, our Mighty God, and yet in your love for us, you understand our need to belong. Help us find peace as we focus on our belonging to You today. During insecure moments, help us to look to you to satisfy, to fill us rather than reaching for the world's quick fixes that increase the ache of our souls.

Digging Deeper:
How can you take some of the words you read today and turn them back into a prayer to the Lord?

DECEMBER 8

Only do not rebel against
the LORD.
And do not be afraid of
the people of the land,
because we will swallow
them up.
Their protection is gone,
but the LORD is with us.
Do not be afraid of them.
Numbers 14:9

The Hebrews arrive at the border of the promise land (the first time), and they send 12 spies to scout out the land for forty days. Just as the Lord has promised, it is lush and bountiful. Yet, the people of the land are mighty, some are even near giants. Ten of the twelve spies were terrified and spread fear among the people to not go and take the land God promised them.

At this moment, Caleb and Joshua, the only two spies with hope, spoke to the assembled people these words. Do not be afraid of them…the Lord is with us. The people compared the battle ahead to their own weakness while Caleb and Joshua compared the battle to God's strength. Sadly, the people went their own way and followed their fear. Caleb and Joshua led the next generation into the same promise land forty years later.

I would like to ask us the same question they were met with years ago. Do you compare your struggles to your own weakness or to God's mighty power and understanding? When God is with us, who can defeat us? With God at our side, what giants will tremble and fall?

Daily Prayer:
Lord God, we face giants each day of our lives. Please walk ahead of us in battle and give us faith like Joshua and Caleb to see our struggles compared to your mighty strength rather than our own weakness. Give us the courage to believe you truly can bring victory and freedom.

Digging Deeper: In your life today, what giants loom over you and cause you to shake with fear? Take some time to rest in the fact that God Almighty is with you in that battle you face today. Let's invite him to take the reins and lead on.

DECEMBER 9

Be strong and
courageous.
Do not be terrified;
do not be discouraged,
for the LORD your
God will be with you
wherever you go.
Joshua 1:9

Forty years have passed since Joshua and Caleb first explored the promised land and the people rebelled against God. They have wandered in the desert for forty long, sandy years, waiting for God's timing to bring them into their future home. They have finally arrived to enter the land.

At this moment, God speaks to Joshua. The gist of God's message...do not be afraid; be strong and courageous; I will go with you wherever you go.

What jumps out at me is how many times God tells him to not be afraid. Even with great faith, one can still battle great fear. It's a daily struggle to lay down our fears, take up courage, and remind ourselves that God is with us. Our fears urgently plea to be heard and followed, but when we are walking along where God leads, he will lift our heads and guide us in paths of victory.

Shortly after God speaks to Joshua, the people conquer their most feared opponent, Jericho. They hardly have to fight at all. They walk around with God, blow horns, and shout at the top of their lungs...nothing their own understanding would have led them to do. But with God, nothing is impossible. With God, impenetrable walls crumble, giants fall, and victories come in the most unexpected ways! Let's take courage and lay down fear today. Let's remember who leads us to victory and walks with us each and every step of the way. God is with us today, my friends! I am so thankful for Emmanuel!

Daily Prayer:
Father, lift our heads to see you when we are afraid. You lead us to victory. Help us to trust you even when we want to control.

Digging Deeper:
What do you think God wants you to walk away with more than anything else today from your time in this scripture?

DECEMBER 10

With him is only the

arm of flesh,

but with us is the

LORD our God

to help us and

fight our battles.

2 Chronicles 32:8

King Hezekiah is one of the good kings of Judah. The king of Assyria lays siege to the city of Jerusalem during Hezekiah's reign. Hezekiah quickly sets to work, diligently getting the city ready for battle. When he assembles all his leaders and soldiers, he speaks these works to them. "Be strong and courageous. Do not be afraid or discouraged because of the king of Assyria and the vast army with him, for there is a greater power with us than with him." Sound familiar? Again and again, we are reminded in the Old Testament that God fights his people's battles. He is the one who brings the victory to his people, despite absurd odds. The people are told to have courage when their eyes scan the vast army and fear creeps in. The King of Assyria only has the strength of people on his side, but God is on the side of Judah!

As the siege continues, the Assyrians fling insult after insult at God and try their best to terrify the people. Hezekiah and Isaiah pray together and the Lord answers mightily! The Word says that God sent and angel and annihilated all the fighting men, officers, and leaders of the Assyrian army. Their king returns home in disgrace. God brought peace to Hezekiah and Judah. What can we take away from this story for our lives? Let's be like Hezekiah and walk uprightly before the Lord. Let's do the work before us…preparing for battle…and when life gets tough, let's hit our knees together.

Daily Prayer:
Lord, in the struggles we face daily, we need you. Help us to walk rightly with you and to come to you first when trouble hits. Father, in you we have power greater than any enemy. Grow our faith to see that victory rests solely in your hands, not our own.

Digging Deeper:
In what way is this scripture particularly meaningful to you?

DECEMBER 11

God is within her;

she will not fall;

God will help her

at the break of day...

The LORD Almighty is

with us; the God of

Jacob is our fortress.

Psalm 46:5,7

Can I just say that Psalm 46 has become my new favorite! If you have the time today, sit with the whole psalm. Emmanuel is all over it! I could talk about this psalm for days...so hard to narrow down a focus for us today. The context of this Psalm reminds me of the battle between king Hezekiah and the Assyrians. Jerusalem is threatened. Daybreak was a common time of battle back then. The psalmist declares that God is within her. I know that this refers to Jerusalem, but it's so rare to see "her" in the Bible. It just catches my attention and I want to put my name in here...anyone else with me, ladies?!

With the Holy Spirit dwelling in us, I feel like we can indeed take this to mean us! God is within each of us! We will not fall. He will help us at the break of day! I struggle with anxiety and at times, my mornings can feel like an uphill battle, feeling overwhelmed and like I'm failing before I step out of bed. This verse is one I want to commit to memory and say on those tough days...God is within me! I will not fall! God will help me as the battles surround me! He is with me! He is my fortress! Let's walk into this busy, often overwhelming and sweet Christmas season today with that confidence!

Daily Prayer:
Father, Emmanuel, thank you for the power of your Holy Spirit in us as a river of life. Thank you that you keep us from falling, that you fight our battles with us and for us. Thank you that our souls are safe in your hands. We ask that you'd give us a peace that passes understanding in this hectic season. Help us to love on the people in our lives with your love and rest in the powerful stillness of your presence.

Digging Deeper:
What do you feel God speaking to you through this passage in particular today?

DECEMBER 12

He tends his flock like a

shepherd: he gathers

the lambs in his arms

and carries them

close to his heart;

he gently leads

those that have young.

Isaiah 40:11

Two days in a row of favorite verses. This one I consider my mama verse. Oh, how I love the sweet gentleness of our Savior described here. Our good shepherd does not beat his sheep into submission. He lifts them in his arms and carries them against his chest. I imagine the lamb resting its soft head against his chest and hearing the lulling thump-thump of his heart beat. I want to be that lamb. (insert a deep breath here).

Then it continues. He gently leads us mamas (and papas) who have young. Gently. Don't we need to be led gently? We are so hard on ourselves...okay at least I am. Opinions about mothering jab at us at every turn...sleeping, feeding, potty training, homework battles, screen time, the list goes on, but I'll stop there cuz I don't want to send any new mamas into a panic attack! Jesus knows us mamas and he knows our sweet (or sometimes not so sweet!) lambs. He gently leads us. Oh, how I need that today. Oh, how I am thankful that he knows my kiddos and their strengths and struggles. Rest in his leading you today, sweet mama. He's got you and your people.

Daily Prayer:
Father, thank you for being our gentle shepherd, caring for our babies and leading us mamas. We need your presence with us today. Thank you for continually reminding us this month of your being near us, with us, within us and of your mighty power. This mom-life can be overwhelming. We need you to guide us. Show us the way to go as we parent our kids, no matter what stage of life they are in.

Digging Deeper:
How does this scripture relate to a prayer request you've had lately?

DECEMBER 13

When the Samaritans
came to him, they
urged him to stay
with them, and he
stayed two days.
John 4:40

For the next few days I want to focus on Jesus being with people throughout his earthly life. He is our Emmanuel. God became human and fully understood the human struggle, our cares, our joys, our battles, our grief and pain. This week, let's focus on Emmanuel in action!

Jesus and his disciples journey from a feast in Jerusalem back to Galilee. Most Jews avoid the route they take since it passes through Samaria, the land of their enemy. When they first arrive in Samaria, the disciples leave Jesus at a well to go into town for food. Meanwhile Jesus talks with a lonely woman who came to draw water at the heat of the day. We find out that she has had five husbands and in currently living with a man. Jesus doesn't rebuke her or shame her. Instead he offers her eternal life and declares to her that he is the Messiah.

She brings out the town to see him and they beg him to stay. Not only is the one conversation against cultural and religious regulations, he has compassion on this village and stays with them for two full days. Jesus is not just for the seemingly perfect church ladies. He is with us in our messes, in our shame and regrets. He lifts our faces and joins with us in our loneliness. Let us open our broken places to him and allow him to fill us with his living water too!

Daily Prayer:
Lord Jesus, you know all the messes of our and you love us anyway. Help us today to loosen our fears and let you heal our most broken places. I pray we'd find freedom from shame and hope for the path and purpose you have for each of us.

Digging Deeper:
Talk to God concerning this section of Scripture. What concerns, joys, fears… did this section raise that you can pour out to God today?

DECEMBER 14

"Neither do I condemn you," Jesus declared. "Go now and leave your life of sin."

John 8:11

Just like yesterday, we have a story of a woman filled with shame being met with the compassion of Emmanuel. The teachers of the law drag a woman caught in the very act of adultery out before Jesus in order to trick him. They trap him between their laws and the Roman law. If he declares her worthy of stoning, he'll have to answer to the Romans. If he doesn't tell them to stone her, he'll have to answer to the Jews for breaking the law. Instead, he bends down and writes in the dirt and says that those without sin should throw the first stone. When he looks up, the mob is gone and the woman is left standing alone.

He evaded their trap and could have gone on his way, but he chooses to interact with her. I imagine her standing there in a bedsheet or with a dress halfway hanging off her. Vulnerable, alone, scoffed at, used by the teachers to trick Jesus, utterly exposed. He looks up at her and talks with her. I imagine his eyes communicating a gleaming love and worth and value that she's never experienced before. Compassion embodied. His response is grace and truth. He doesn't condemn her or condone her actions. He loves on her, showers grace, and shows her the way to proceed…leave the life of sin.

Daily Prayer:
Jesus, thank you for loving us with your grace and not leaving us alone to deal with our messes. Thank you for defending us, for coming along side us. Help us to leave the life of sin that pulls at us.

Digging Deeper:
How do you imagine her life changed after this horrible and grace-filled experience?

DECEMBER 15

"What do you
want me
to do for you?"
Jesus asked him.
Mark 10:51

As Jesus and his disciples are leaving Jericho, a blind man named Bartimaeus shouts for Jesus to help him. He does not relent despite the crowds hushing him. Even more, he calls out to Jesus for mercy. Jesus stops and calls for him. The very people who'd shushed him must have led him before the Lord. I imagine him standing there awkwardly and in expectation of a miracle. Then comes the question that stills my heart. "What do you want me to do for you?" Bart wants to see. Because of Jesus's power and Bart's faith, his eyes are opened! His first sight…his Savior, full of joy and compassion and power!

A Bible study leader asked us a few years back to close our eyes and imagine Jesus looking down at us, cupping our chin in his hands and asking this very same question: What do you want me to do for you? My instant response was healing for my dad who had battled Multiple Sclerosis for decades. Then my heart ached as I imagined Jesus still gazing at me. My dad was still sick, despite thousands of prayers. Jesus, I went on, I want your comfort, your peace, your healing of this ache that lumps in my throat, and for the ability to trust you when I don't like your answers. Well, my dad, is now fully healed, in heaven. A new lump forms in my throat as I miss him, but a smile grows when I think of his healthy body, mind and voice.

Daily Prayer:
Jesus, thank you for knowing our hearts, for knowing what we need, and yet asking us anyway. Lord, we pray that you'd help us to stand before you honestly and ask for our deepest desire. Guide us in our response to your answer. Thank you that you pour out compassion on us. Thank you for meeting us in this place of vulnerable need.

Digging Deeper:
How would you answer Jesus today if he lifted your chin to his eyes and asked you to share your deepest desire? Start the conversation and see where it leads.

DECEMBER 16

But the Counselor, the Holy Spirit, whom the Father will send in my name, will teach you all things and remind you of everything I have said to you. Peace I leave with you; my peace I give you. I do not give to you as the world gives. Do not let your hearts be troubled, and do not be afraid.

John 14:26-27

As Jesus nears the end of his time with his disciples, he begins preparing them for what life will look like when he heads back home to Heaven. I love knowing what to expect in the next part of my day or season of life. Are you that way too? I love that Jesus recognizes this need we have to know what's around the corner.

He introduces his disciples to the concept of the Holy Spirit, the Counselor. Look at what the Spirit will do for them (and does for us)! The Spirit will teach them all things and remind them of everything Jesus said to them.

Can you imagine remembering every word Jesus spoke to them over the three years they hung out together? I imagine this is how the gospels were written. The Spirit called to mind with crystal clarity each teaching of Jesus so the authors could record them for us today.

There is more than that though. Jesus promises his peace would be with his followers. Worldly peace rests in circumstances. Jesus's peace rests in our hearts regardless of our situation. It is a product of His Spirit filling us rather than what's going on around us.

In this world we will indeed have trouble, but Jesus promises to be with us, to give us peace, and to remind us of his truth. That is certainly good news!

Daily Prayer:
Lord Jesus, thank you for your peace and your Spirit's reminding and teaching us. Open our minds to focus on what you would have us learn today. Open our hearts to feel the deep peace you alone bring.

Digging Deeper:
In what way is this passage particularly meaningful to you?

DECEMBER 17

And surely,

I am with you

always,

to the very

end of the age.

Matthew 28:20

Jesus's last words to his disciples: I AM WITH YOU ALWAYS. Emmanuel until the end and beyond. He gives them their assignment…go and make disciples, baptizing them, and teaching them. I imagine their excitement for their purpose and mission, but terrified as well. They just witnessed Jesus's death at the hands of the Jews and Romans.

If I had been on that mountain with them, I think I'd have felt a bit like Moses when God threatened to not continue with them. Like, "Hang on a minute. I cannot do this without you here, without your power, courage, and presence." Jesus knows the hearts of people. He knew what Moses needed way back when, he knows what his disciples need, and he knows today what you and I need…his Presence.

One thing has stuck with me in this study…when God is with a person or group, there is mighty power shown. This promise extends to us…to the very end of the age. Jesus is with us through the Holy Spirit! His power and might and wisdom and compassion are all available to us in what he has called us to…working, mothering, ministering, caring for parents, teaching. Let's ask him to come into our lives and display his perpetual Presence.

Daily Prayer:
Lord Jesus, thank you for not leaving us alone to carry on the purpose you've given to us. Thank you for the power of your Presence in our lives. We pray that we would be consciously aware of you with us in each moment. In the callings you've given, help us to trust you to provide what we need and lean not on our own understanding. Thank you for being our Emmanuel.

Digging Deeper:
In what way is this section particularly meaningful to you?

DECEMBER 18

But you will receive power when the Holy Spirit comes on you; and you will be my witnesses in Jerusalem, and in Judea and Samaria, and to the ends of the earth." Acts 1:9

Like yesterday, we are still a top the mountain, as Jesus is about to disappear into the clouds. Imagine the disciples' fear and grief at saying good-bye. He's given them an enormous task. I imagine they question their abilities, fearing the obstacles that lay before them.

Then, Jesus directs them, "Stay in Jerusalem. Wait for the gift my Father has promised, which you have heard me speak about. For John baptized with water, but in a few days, you will be baptized with the Holy Spirit."

Can you see the confused glances bouncing around the group as they try to comprehend this?

He continues, "But you will receive power when the Holy Spirit comes on you; and you will be witnesses in Jerusalem, and in all Judea and Samaria, and to the ends of the earth."

Here, I imagine relief settles into them. They begin counting on the best present of the season. They will go from being next to Jesus to having his very Spirit inside them, empowering them, reminding them, encouraging them, as they take his message to the ends of the earth. They have a purpose and mission to fulfill and will have the means to accomplish it with the powerful Spirit at work in their very souls. As do we, my friends.

Daily Prayer:
Lord Jesus, we ask you today to fill us each with a new measure of your Holy Spirit. May your power and goodness bubble up in us to overflowing today as we seek to be your witnesses where we are today.

Digging Deeper:
What do you think God wants you to walk away with more than anything else today from your time in this scripture?

DECEMBER 19

They saw what seemed
to be tongues of fire
that separated and
came to rest on each
of them. All of them
were filled with
the Holy Spirit.
Acts 2:3

In the week since Jesus ascended into Heaven, his followers meet continually in the Temple in Jerusalem. They worship and praise God together.

This day, as they come together in one place, a strange sound like the rushing of the wind fills the whole place where they are sitting. On top of each person's head what seems like a tongue of fire comes to rest. In that moment they are each filled with the Holy Spirit, the best gift of Christmas. They begin to miraculously speak God's wonders in languages they do not actually know how to speak. Yet, in Jerusalem, people are assembled from all over the Roman world. These folks hear these unschooled men speaking of God's wonders in their own languages.

Have you ever visited a place where you hardly heard your language spoken? It can be lonely and jarring to listen to speech you cannot understand. These travelers may have felt the same way. Then, they suddenly pick up the sound of their mother tongue and their heads whip around searching for a familiar face. Instead they gaze upon these uneducated men from Galilee speaking their language. God's Spirit poured out brought unity of language for his glory. Peter then stands up and boldly proclaims the good news. The fearful crew has power in the Spirit!

Daily Prayer:
Lord Jesus, may your Holy Spirit rest upon us and work through us mightily. Wash away our fears and help us to step into the purpose you have for us this day, right where we are.

Digging Deeper:
After reading this passage, what questions do you have? Write them down and try to answer them.

DECEMBER 20

Now the dwelling of God is with men, and he will live with them. They will be his people and God himself will be their God. He will wipe every tear from their eyes. There will be no more death or mourning or crying or pain, for the old order of things has passed away.
Revelation 21:3

Near the end of the book of Revelation, John sees the new heaven and the new earth. The old order of things has passed away and God is making all things new. From his throne, God calls out the words of our verse today.

I hear echoes of our past devotions in this verse. God first dwelt with the people in the tabernacle, meeting with Moses there. The next sentence reminds me of our belonging to God and his belonging to us. Throughout this month, when I've turned my mind to "God and I belong to each other," peace and calm and confidence wash over me. Our worth rests in that belonging no matter how poorly or well we perform in our daily tasks. The last two sentences of this verse take my thoughts back to Jesus with the shamed and forgotten. His compassion pours out to us.

Oh, how I long for God to wipe every tear from our eyes and end death and grief and broken hearts. This season is yet to come. We are in still in what C.S. Lewis referred to as the Shadowlands, a valley mixed with painful grief and great joy. I am thankful that as we continue in this valley, we are not alone. Emmanuel understands our pain. He lived it. He offers us his compassion, love, grace, and power. His presence is our peace and sure foundation.

Daily Prayer:
Emmanuel, thank you for a glimpse at the new order of life! And thank you that while we wait in our tears and suffering, that you are with us. Thank you for understanding our pain and grief. We pray that you'd open our hearts to your presence, the joy of being with you in every circumstance that surround us.

Digging Deeper:
How would you react to God wiping away your tears?

greatful.

DECEMBER 21

The Holy Spirit will
come upon you, and
the power of
the Most High will
overshadow you,
so the holy one
to be born
will be called
the Son of God.
Luke 1:35

As we approach Christmas, let's turn our focus toward Emmanuel, even in the nativity.

To Mary, a poor teenage girl from a village far from anywhere important, God sends an angel to announce the most defining moment of her life. She is to mother the Son of God! The angel's words "The Holy Spirit will come upon you" and "overshadow you" have always seemed mysterious to me. I really don't know what they mean except that by the creative life-giving power of God, cells inside Mary began to divide and cleave and grow into God. When I was pregnant with my kids, I loved getting to feel them move inside me. I loved imagining what they would be like and how life would go for them. Can you imagine knowing that for nine months, God himself is growing inside you? That it is God who is kicking you in the ribs, God who makes you crave bread and have a crazy sense of smell. Mary's baby bump that brings ridicule and judgement from her community is really her growing God belly.

Now, we are not going to be pregnant with God, but what if we allowed him to interrupt our lives with his call and basked in his perpetual Presence as Mary did? How would that change your self-worth, your inner monologue, your responses to your family and community? It would sure change me, grow my confidence, and give me a peace that is solid despite the struggles of each day.

Daily Prayer:
Lord, thank you for coming as a fragile baby, for taking on our humanity, for understanding us. We pray that you'd help us submit to your interruptions in our lives. Help us to let you fill us with your Spirit and re-make us into your children. Help us to be more like Mary today.

Digging Deeper:
How would living this out change your life?

DECEMBER 22

Joseph,

son of David,

do not be

afraid.

Matthew 1:20

I've never really taken the time to take Joseph's perspective. He's a grown man whose teenage wife to be is scandalously pregnant. To make things worse, she's saying God got her pregnant. In his "kindness", he plans to divorce her quietly rather than making a big deal in their tiny village of Nazareth. (Not sure small-town life is ever quietly done...pretty sure all would know and talk anyway). Joseph must be hurt, upset and think Mary has gone CRA-zy! Then the angel appears to him in a dream to tell him that the baby is indeed from God and to give him the name Jesus. When he wakes up, Joseph is a changed man. I wonder how his view of Mary changed in that moment, from loose lunatic to chosen mother of God's own Son. I bet he was in awe of that and respected her more for it. He instantly obeys the angel's message. Takes Mary to be his wife right away, no more doubts.

He accepts this new shared adventure with Mary. He submits to the interruption of God in their life plans. Up until this point, I imagine he had a life path laid out before them in Nazareth...carpentry, small village life, kids, family, obscurity. In the blink of an eye that cozy plan is upended and they spend the next years traveling to Bethlehem, Egypt, and finally back to their home town. Joseph becomes Jesus's earthly protector. From here on out he follows each call of the angel in his dreams. I want to be more like Joseph.

Daily Prayer:
Lord Jesus, help us to be more like Joseph, willing to change and flex to you and loving those you bring into our care.

Digging Deeper:
What is God expecting from Joseph? Does he expect the same from us?

DECEMBER 23

I bring you good news that will bring great joy to all people.

Luke 2:10

Today let's focus on the shepherds. It's an ordinary quiet star-filled night in the fields outside of Bethlehem. Maybe this group of men are snoozing or talking or laughing around a fire. They are on the lower rungs of the social ladder, poor, dirty, looked down upon.

Suddenly the sky above these rough me explodes with heavenly light and song. They are invited to see the king of all kings…in a place they would feel quite at home, a stable filled with dirty animals and a humble couple.

I love the beauty of this humble start to Jesus' life. The King of all creation first reveals his glory to the everyday, the overlooked, and the lowly.

He breaks open the darkness and his glorious Light shines for each and every one of us.

Daily Prayer:
Lord God, thank you for sharing your birth with the lowly people of Bethlehem. Thank you that you come for each of us, not just those in power and influence. You value each person. Shine your bright light into our hearts today and fill us with the confidence of knowing that it was for even us that you descended from heaven to be born at Christmas.

Digging Deeper:
In what way does the angels message and concert for the shepherds speak to you?

DECEMBER 24

So Joseph also went up from the town of Nazareth in Galilee to Judea, to Bethlehem the town of David, because he belonged to the house and line of David. He went there to register with Mary, who was pledged to be married to him and was expecting a child. While they were there, the time came for the baby to be born, and she gave birth to her firstborn, a son. She wrapped him in cloths and placed him in a manger, because there was no guest room available for them.
Luke 2:4-7

A hush falls over me as I wake up on the 24th. In our family we have an anniversary and a birthday in this week. The 24th is a day of thoughtful celebration. This to me is the day when we can focus primarily on Jesus, the newborn king, our Emmanuel. In the blink of the night, presents will explode from beneath our tree and laughter and playing and toys and that Christmas afternoon low will descend as all the fun begins to wrap up.

In this moment, let's hush and enter the quiet murmuring of the stable. Jesus, the King of the universe, God of Heaven and Earth, just became a baby. He took on a body and instead of coming in as a super-hero of sorts, he takes the most dependent form: an infant, and a poor one at that. He was most likely born in a pile of hay with pungent scents of farm animals wafting over him.

Why would God choose this? Our Father passionately longs to be close to us. Jesus's mission was to not only take our humanity but also the punishment for how we fall short. Because of his humble birth and life, we have a God who fully understands us. Because of his death, we are forgiven. Finally, because of his rising from the dead, we have life forever with him!

Daily Prayer:
Jesus, thank you for being with us, for taking on skin and bones, and splinters, and sore muscles for us to feel understood. Help us to find quiet and calm today to focus our hearts on your Presence with us. Thank you, our Emmanuel. Thank you.

Digging Deeper:
What strikes you most from reading this passage today?

ABOUT THE AUTHOR

Maggie Greenway is an artist and devotional writer. She
loves studying the Word as she hand-letters and paints
works of art for her online devotionals. You can connect
with her on Instagram at @shepenstruth. Her artwork and
daily devotionals are available online at shepenstruth.com.
She lives near Seattle with her husband Chris, their three
kids, and their dog.

Made in the USA
Monee, IL
06 December 2019